CROSSOVER

CROSSOVER:
AN AMERICAN BIO

BY CARMAN MOORE

gpc
GRACE PUBLISHING COMPANY

Published in the United States of America by
The Grace Publishing Company (USA)
Manufactured in the United States of America

Back Cover Photo: Pearl Perkins
Cover Design: Jeff Chen

Library of Congress Catalog Card Number: 2011929734

Library of Congress Cataloging-in-Publication Data

Moore, Carman
Crossover: An American Bio/Carman Moore

p. cm

ISBN: 1877807-79-6
ISBN: 978-1877807794

1. Moore, Carman—Bio   2. 20th century.   3. Race relations—
4. Middle class.   5. African-American male.   6. Music Critic —
7. Composer.   8. Conductor.   9. Writer —   United States

10 9 8 7 6 5 4 3 2 1

DEDICATION:

To those who have dared to cross the lines established by those who fear to cross the lines.

ESPECIALLY:
Hall Overton
Frederick Douglass
Dante Alighieri
John Milton
Martin Luther
Martin Luther King
Grandma Franklin
Grandpa Franklin
Benjamin Franklin
Louis Armstrong
Duke Ellington
The Modern Jazz Quartet
Charlie Parker
Jalal al-Din Muhammad Rumi
Thelonious Monk
Franz Josef Haydn

Ludwig van Beethoven
The Beatles
Anwar el Sadat
Barack Obama

ACKNOWLEDGEMENTS:

Thanks to Mom who made reading and writing delightful and music natural. Appreciation to late great composer/teacher Hall Overton, who decided to lavish time and attention on my notion to become a real composer. Thanks to Kyle Jones for constant support and for archiving and digitizing my work. Special thanks to Skymusic Ensemble members past and present, including: Eric Johnson, Ken Bichel, Leroy Jenkins, Marianna Rosett, Sam Rivers, Gordon Gottlieb, Kitty Hay, Premik Russell Tubbs, Eli Fountain, Mark Heinemann, Charles Burnham, Elliott Randall, Dale Kleps, Linda Wetherill, and Daisy Jopling...whose disparate world-class genius made my crossing over irresistible...and to Caterina Bertolotto and Angela Verdurmen who joined their wonderful art forms with ours. Thanks to the rockers of the powerful new Skyband. Heartfelt appreciation to brilliant life-long friends Alvin Singleton, Robert Cram, and Maryse Maynard to whom I entrusted and from whom I received invaluable manuscript commentary. Thanks to the versatile and gifted Billielee Mommer for her ever-ready ideas and life lessons. Propers to Ishmael Reed for an example of gift and courage. Thanks to my marvelous sons Martin and Justin (and my grands Ally and Justin, Jr.) who have unwaveringly advised me and kept my heart open. Thanks for gifted lifer Barbara Pecarich for constant support.

Thanks for incisive and loving photography by Pearl Perkins and the late Hal Wilson. And finally thanks with heart full to my Guide, the brilliant editor Grace Adams, who decided that I must open my life as a book, views that project as a gift to generations to come, and has worked hard to make it real.

INTRODUCTION:

"CROSSOVER" is a music-world concept meaning appealing to and/or being accepted by an audience other than the one you're normally creating or performing for. It's considered a positive, both in terms of sales and expanded expectations. You can unexpectedly grow from it. At its most powerful it can result in the creation of entirely new cultures.

The first crossover of concern to me and my life involved one from a place in Africa, across the Atlantic Ocean, and into the American New World. Upwards of 15 million Africans crossed alive (so many started but never arrived), and an adventure resulting in me began. And to be sure, some 30,000 years ago my "red" component crossed the ice bridge of the Bering Straits into this continent, while relatively  recently my third, European component found his or her way from somewhere in the British Isles to this same America---land of crossover.

As I grew up, whatever mixture I might have been genetically, I and people who looked like me were considered Black. Along with that consideration went a series of well-known treatments and implied obligations by the White majority. So as a youth I found myself dealing with certain questions about self which demanded answers:

1.) Was there something inherently wrong about being black? If there was, I was determined to either fix it or accept it and adjust to it as some kind of chronic disease.

2.) Was there a problem with my looks or lovability? But I certainly was loved with looks approved of by my mother and grandmother, both of whom I decided were women of good taste.

3.) Did being black mean a deficit of brain power, since admittedly African-Americans as a group were not doing well in school or getting into colleges at an appropriate rate. But with Slavery--- an institution that routinely denied slaves the right to learn to read---behind us by very few generations, what could you expect? (Though my own brilliant grandfather, whose mother was a slave, was one of the first post-Slavery black college graduates, his I.Q. clearly stratospheric beyond that of most Americans black or white I knew of).

4.) Even the question of athletic ability and manliness existed, since professional sports when I was a child, with the exception of boxing (Jesse Owens made his mark in track as an amateur) were denied to blacks.

So I set out to explore those questions, when appropriate, in my own life. And to be sure, I was clearly not the only one exploring, because racial barriers were falling right and left just as I grew into manhood.

CROSSOVER is my Bio—the bio of an Agent of Change.
It has been inspired by family members, friends, and admired ones who have broken away from the conventionally obvious.

My personal motto from the beginning has been "Don't try to predict me. You'll just be wasting your time." – **Carman Moore**

Carman Moore Conducting Naomi Itami
in soprano aria from Mass for the 21stCentury

CONTENTS

CROSSOVER:
AN AMERICAN BIO

Elyria, Ohio 1942

ANCESTORS

My Grandpa Moore was feisty, imaginative, short and funny…a tireless practical joker. He liked his whiskey and never went to any church that I know of. He lived across a field from our house in Elyria, Ohio and loved my visits as a toddler, and as I sat on his porch, I would watch New York Central railroad trains go by on the way to Cleveland or Who Knew (maybe somewhere  I might go someday?). I remember all that to this day, even though Grandpa Ross Moore died when I was 5 years old. I recently read his 1910 Census entry: born in Sheperdstown, West Virginia (not far from Antietam Creek)..race listed as "mulatto." And recently I've heard that he'd been a well-regarded jockey in his youth. The Moore side was athletic. My uncle Lawrence "Tiger" Moore, WWII vet, was a top middle-weight boxer in Northern Ohio, and my younger uncles, Tommy and Brook (he visited Brooklyn once) home from World War II, I remember as lightning-fast and excellent and obsessive about playing baseball.

Grandma Moore died before I came along. I still wonder what she was like. Maternal Grandma Texana Paige Franklin's father was a Creek Indian who built fences for a living and crossed back and forth between his family in the wilds of Eastern Alabama and his black Christian wife and family in Burnt Corn, Alabama, presumably even changing attire on the way. He was the elemental cross-over man in my family, for sure. Grandma told us often of when he would take

her out there to meet "his people." She said she was actually afraid of her (heathen) paternal kin---"they could sit on their hair," she would exclaim. Grandma said that her mother Asenas Johnson Paige was a 16-year old slave working in "a big house" when the Freedom Bell rang. The Franklin side was religious with God deep in their hearts and ways. Grandma sang spirituals on the porch in Lorain, Ohio as she peeled potatoes or sewed kids' clothes. She smoked a pipe.

Grandpa Franklin, believe it or not named Benjamin Franklin, was ahead of his time…the brilliant son of a mother born in Slavery, he graduated in 1904 from Tuskegee Institute, as therefore one of the first post-Slavery black American college graduates. My Grandpa, who always described himself as meek—as in "the meek shall inherit the earth"--- majored in religion and philosophy. His education included reading Emerson, Thoreau, and the major theologians of the day. Among his professors were George Washington Carver and Booker T. Washington.

Correctly speaking "good English" (King James Bible-inflected) remained a life-long value of his. Grandpa's dear college friend (one whom he privately called "a heathen") was a gifted pianist who taught piano (classical) to my mother and older sister. I must thank this heathen for the chain of events that have gotten me to where I am today. Grandpa's gentleness made him leave the South and its degradation of black folks as soon as possible. He packed his books and pulled his family out of Alabama and headed for the Northern Ohio steel town of Lorain. But even there his education and excellent mind were wasted, and he chose to spend his life working on a nearby farm and reading and writing for pleasure after work was done.

Grandpa Franklin preached occasionally (maybe a bit intellectually over our heads) in our little New Hope church. One thing I recall is his instructing us to "be nice to Jews, because they are God's chosen people." Of course there seemed to be scant few Jews in Lorain or Elyria to practice that on. Grandpa was mysterious and fascinating. I used to follow him around a lot. He died in 1977.

Grandma and Grandpa saved up and on a quiet little street in Lorain, bought a house, creating a one-acre garden with chickens in back. And they were perforce vegetarians—organic only, mind you—but didn't know it (couldn't afford meat except for chicken on Sundays after church). Grandma was an astoundingly gifted cook. You could get high on her custard pies or barbecued ribs for sure. They also bought an old upright piano for their living room. Grandma proceeded to insist that all her children and grandchildren learn to play a musical instrument. I am clear that it was because she selfishly just loved to hear people play music. And in Lorain Grandma and Grandpa established The New Hope A.M.E. Zion Church in a rented union hall (Of course it was attended by virtually no one but the family). I can still hear Grandma saying  to each of us grandkids, "make something of your self." In Ohio she could say it knowing it didn't have to be just wishful thinking. I can only imagine the contrast of them living in relative peace in Lorain, Ohio compared to what they left in Alabama where black people had to be wary of white people as dangerous to their lives and crushing to their dignity.

GROWING UP

My hometown of Elyria, Ohio was a basically white town with a small African-American section in what they called the South End. We Moores lived in a mixed-race pocket near factories and the excellent McKinley School, where I and all 7 younger siblings  went and where my father Claude attended through the 4th grade---before running away to join a circus feeding animals (maybe preparing him for life with all of us). My father, once-returned to Elyria, signed on basically for a hard-labor life at the Elyria Foundry.... made friends with co-worker Mike the Magyar, a true Christian who would bring stuffed cabbage and paprikash to our large family after Hungarian weddings, wakes, or such. Since my mother used to make spaghetti with ketchup for sauce, Mike's gifts must have been our first experience of international cuisine. In those days most Elyrians didn't "eat out," but we all knew there were certain restaurants in town where blacks should not even try to go and be served.

And talk about cross-over, legend has it that my father was out fishing and drinking with an Italian-American buddy Carmine the night I was born and ended up assigning a version of his name to me. Claude Leroy Moore, my father, was a husky, muscular, and very generous man. He worked for some 25 years at the Elyria Foundry swinging sledge hammers and manually polishing the surfaces of large metal casings. Like old Ross, my dad liked his whiskey but drank solely on weekends. A lot...he was a weekend alcoholic. One thing I've always appreciated about him was the fact that he'd often take me and my sister Claudette as little squirts down to his favorite bar on West Avenue and show us off just because he loved and admired us. We hadn't done anything notable at all. He loved children, and it's a darned good thing---he fathered 8 of us.

My mother Jessie Lee was a model housewife and like her parents, never touched alcohol. An accomplished pianist, she played all kinds of classics and boogie-woogie but obsessively Duke Ellington. We always had an upright piano, and she would routinely rush over to the keys and play something before dashing after the next toddler or cooking or laundering or... And there was a light-classical radio program every morning on Cleveland's WGAR whose theme music was a charming little Haydn minuet. I realize now that it was no accident that it played every morning as I awoke to go to school. That Haydn was my wake-up reality. Mom was planning something.

...EARLY SCHOOLING

Public education in Ohio was excellent when I went to school with top teachers among WWII veterans returning, going to colleges under the GI Bill of Rights, and plowing their educations into public school teaching. Music, too, with football a virtual state religion, received enormous support probably because every Ohio town wanted to field at least a first-rate marching band.

I grew up just as WWII was ending and Civil Rights activities were blossoming into an unstoppable movement. I remember when in high school a black friend (Kenny Logan...who also became a local basketball star) told me excitedly "there's this music over in Cleveland called rhythm and blues, and black people are singing and playing it." And post-War sports were a very big player in our lives. On a national level most of what we knew of African-American athletes was about boxers---Sugar Ray Robinson and wow! Joe Louis---and sprinters such as Jesse Owens (from Ohio State University). Then suddenly Jackie Robinson burst into America's pastime, followed almost immediately by Larry Doby 20 miles away in Cleveland with the Indians. Older black people were euphoric. Kids didn't quite get what was the big deal.

Tennis seemed totally white, so I decided to become a tennis player and rose to become the

Elyria H.S. tennis team's number-one man. I learned because someone gave us an old wooden Slazenger and a ball, and my uncles taught me whatever they thought a tennis stroke should be in the middle of the street. I was already a regular at the Elyria Public Library and took out and kept out "How To Play Better Tennis" by Bill Tilden ("better" than what?" I was frequently asked). The local tennis court functioned as an  informal instrument of racial integration with respect granted whoever could learn to hit a respectable backhand. White Southerner Leroy Johnson, the best player, becoming nearly-as-accomplished black Jerry Gaines's best friend. Throughout life subsequently I've found tennis a door to meeting very special friends, among them basketball star Earl Monroe and film legend Robert Redford. I've also played tennis with (and beaten) Dave DeBusschere and Robert Duvall.

Everything society at the time said I wasn't supposed to do, I had to try. Everything I thought society had already decided about me because of my race, I had to subvert. It didn't all work out---I never learned to swim or ice skate very well---but I had to have a go. I worked very hard in school, as well, and maintained high grades and competed consciously with any student who dared to best me in the classroom. Actually all this was only in part that I wanted to reserve my rights of stubbornness. Upon careful hind-sight I now see all that as more having been a means to self knowledge---a way of learning about myself—strengths and weaknesses---what I dared to try and what to steer clear of. I kept getting away with it (and enjoying the ride). As early as 4th Grade I got myself hired at a local butcher shop BAZELY'S MEATS, and as soon as I could see over the counter  I was allowed to wait on customers---which seemed to amuse everybody immensely. With my earnings I not only bought myself a Schwinn balloon-tired bicycle, I also bought myself a shiny-new Selmer trumpet. And I practiced hard on it.

In part because of a taste for things military but probably in the main because of football madness, the state of Ohio was and is band country. And as a result, support for music and first-rate music training have always been high priorities there. At Elyria High I expanded from trumpet and took up the cello and French horn, both owned by the school. After a few lessons on horn, I found myself being the first-chair player in the concert band. The school orchestra needed cellos, so I quick studied cello and soon began playing it in the orchestra. During my senior year, despite a relatively thin command of the cello, I got 3 fellow student string players and a clarinetist to gather daily in a closet-sized room at lunch time, eat fast, and then go to work on pieces by Mozart, Haydn, and others. It was a joy. With graduation approaching, seniors were sent to consult with the Dean of Boys, one Mr. Thourot, a beady-eyed stuffed shirt who had no business advising anybody about anything. Knowing I was applying to colleges---Ohio State and University of Chicago were my main choices---, he urged me to forget about nuclear physics or history or even classical music. He suggested I join some hot jazz band, because black people were known to be good at it. I loved listening to jazz and still do. But his advice was probably crucial to my having chosen the intense study of classical music...majoring on French horn. "Don't try to predict me. You'll just be wasting your time."

Of course I realize how fortunate I have been to have been born and bred at a period of enormous change in race and human-rights matters in America. It was a time when a young black guy might actually be able to follow Grandma's requirement that you make something of yourself.

CM TO COLLEGE AT OSU

So I chose Ohio State University, a state school where with a small scholarship most of my expenses were covered. I was housed and fed in the Stadium Dorms, the first year rooming with a bunch of guys that included All-American and NFL Hall of Fame lineman Jim Parker (who used to call me "Cat Man,"  because I was a musician). I had to come up with no more than $400 for each year as I remember it. Didn't know what to expect from Columbus, Ohio, I'd never been there.

My first year in Columbus I was shocked to experience not being allowed entrance to the (white) downtown YMCA (sic! the Young Men's Christian Association). And I noticed that some white adults there would avoid sitting next to me on buses. So I tended to stay on campus where all was pretty comfortable. Fellow students at the School of Music became my new family, and I'm sure the racist thing got put to rest soon after. I never tested it. White fellow music students seemed to regard jazz and jazz musicians as the hippest thing happening, which meant Miles, Thelonious, Basie, Ellington, Dizzy, and especially MJQ (which had a classical veneer to them). Black J.J. Johnson and

White Kai Winding (J and K) were gods for trombone majors. And, such hip and advanced white jazz men as Stan Kenton, Dave Brubeck, Herbie Mann, Lenny Tristano and company were crossovers from the other side whose music I and many black friends cherished. Turns out that good music can translate perfectly all by itself.

OSU Marching Band

I soon became first-chair horn in the OSU concert band and eventually in the orchestra. And of course I chose to (had to) join the famed OSU Marching Band as both obligation and opportunity. Free football games, that Script Ohio formation, and 2 crazy train trips to Pasadena during cold Ohio winters to play in the Rose Bowl Game were payoffs. Walking towards the stadium one cold November afternoon I found myself alongside

Coach Woody Hayes. Finding that I was a band member, he engaged me in some spirited and delightful conversation. Of course some of us music majors were so cool and into music and the Band as to maybe look down on the football part of the Saturday afternoon ritual, especially during years when the Buckeyes weren't national championship contenders.

OSU MARCHING BAND before a Rose Bowl Game

We were a precise, musically-clean, hard-practicing outfit that felt we won every time we took the field. As a senior I contributed thematic ideas for Marching Band shows upon a few occasions.

It was at the advice of Marching Band arranger Dick Heine that I moved to New York to study composition with his friend the great Hall Overton.

31

Many of us music majors avoided any serious military involvement by joining a School of Music-populated Army Reserve Band. Maybe we couldn't shoot straight, but we could play some mean Sousa and make the grunts wake up and feel like pickin' 'em up and layin' 'em down. During one Reservist summer camp outside Hershey, Pennsylvania 3 classmate/Reservists and I motored off to New York and saw "West Side Story" on Broadway. I never got over it and, of course, have ended up an inveterate New Yorker.

THE NYC '60S--- LEARNING AT JUILLIARD and THE VILLAGE

I graduated but left college with great trepidations. I had no idea where I fit in or how I might be supported. I had gotten no more than a B in my Music Comp course at OSU. But I still had this crazy unsupported notion that I might be supposed to compose, based on the constant sounding of music---music whose origin I could not place--- that would circulate endlessly through my head.

So with hardly a dime in my pocket and Dick Heine's recommendation I contacted Hall Overton and took the next Greyhound to New York. A couple nights at the 34th Street Y and a job acceptance at the N.Y. Public Library (meeting the newly-hired Alvin Singleton), and things began to fall into place. Of course work with Hall began with being brought virtually to tears trying to find his loft near 29th Street and 6th Avenue. I was more than on-time but spent some 2 hours lost until someone pointed out to me that the fancy-named Avenue of the Americas was 6th Avenue. He and I never stopped laughing at that one.

It was fall 1958. After moving to relatives in the Bronx for a short time, I settled in Greenwich

Village and found a room in the Judson Student House of the Judson Church. I began four amazing, full, detailed years of study with Overton followed by 2 years of Masters work at the Juilliard School with first Vincent Persichetti and then Luciano Berio. These three wonders lavished excellent guidance on me during the '60s. Hall started teaching me from scratch all he knew (and I didn't yet know) about the craft of classical composition. My Saturday afternoon at 4 lessons often stretched out so long that I would nod out in the middle. He would plunge on. I soon found out that Hall was not only a first-rate classical composer: he was also a first-rate jazz pianist and teacher of many a star of jazz during that golden period in the music's history. Many an evening he played host to jam sessions in his loft studio attracting almost every major artist in jazz. One Saturday evening, my marathon lesson over, there came a knock on the door, and in walked Thelonious Monk, there to work with Hall on the famous Monk's Big Band at Town Hall concert. Monk was not talking in those days, but he did grunt me a hello and by quietly lingering I heard him and Hall play piano. And I got to shake the hand of Thelonious Monk!

Among my classmates at Juilliard were Itzhak Perlman, Martha Clarke, Joseph Kalichstein, Robert Cram, Pinchas Zuckerman, and gangs of instrumentalists who've since taken over first chairs of major symphony orchestras and chamber groups. Among my teachers were the aforementioned

Persichetti and Berio, Roger Sessions, and the magisterial ear-training teacher Renee Longy. Madame Longy famously had been Leonard Bernstein's ear-training teacher, one who had flunked entire classes at music schools in the past. She might occasionally regale us with such stories as when as a teenager she attended the premiere of Stravinsky's "Rite Of Spring" and witnessed Claude Debussy leaping onto a seat and shouting down naysayers and tomato throwers. But mainly she would torture us with virtually impossible exercises she'd sing and make us write down. This was daily.

So when one morning at the end of my senior year the phone rang and it was Madame, I choked and I cringed thinking "OMG, I failed Ear Training." But glory be, she announced "Mistah Moore, every year I select 2 students who have done especially well to join me at a New York Philharmonic dress rehearsal. Rehearsal begins at 10 a.m. Can you be there?" Stammer stammer--- "Wild horses couldn't keep me away, Madame." By the way, at the rehearsal she grew irritated at Bernstein's conducting of a rhythmically-challenging passage in Brahms' "Second Symphony" almost to the point of demanding they stop and try it again. "That boy never could get those cross rhythms right," Madame murmured loudly. He welcomed her warmly and requested a private work session with her. She took out her appointment book, announcing loudly, "Okay, but some of us have to work for a living." My mother claims that I taught myself to read somewhere between 2 and 3 years. Don't remember, but I've always loved poetry and had written some from 'way young. So, comfortable writing, I talked the quite new Village Voice into letting me start a new-music column (for no or little pay) with focus on new classical music but soon adding jazz and popular music of all kinds. At the time the Voice was entering its glory years of good writing. I soon found myself welcome at almost every concert of new classical music, jazz, or popular and received great bag-loads of what folks used to call "records."

It was the '60s and music had become the main purveyor of philosophy, poetic thought, and physical style. At times it might be Dylan, Hendrix, Grace Slick, Aretha Franklin, the Beatles, James Brown, the Stones, or Marvin Gaye...at others it might be Stravinsky, Berio, Stockhausen, or John Cage. Before Big Business reined all these masters in, music was all, and I got to participate as both critic and creator.

PROFESSIONAL LIFE

The job at the Voice changed my life. Being able to attend any concert I wished for free and being entrusted with critical comment on the strange field of classical new music, I found myself being less afraid to consider myself a music professional. I could also, of course, match my own by ear with all the new pieces being created, both Uptown and Downtown.

CM as an emerging composer, music critic, and curious fellow

Uptown music was centered on left-brained, carefully-crafted pieces, with its notes often derived via mathematical notions themselves the products of Europeans steeped in "serial/12-tone" systems. Derogatorily referred to as "Columbia/Princeton

Axis," Uptown music was not too audience-friendly, especially if that audience were just casually-curious music lovers. Princeton professor/composer the late Milton Babbitt (who once taught Stephen Sondheim) was quoted as saying that he basically composed for his colleagues.

CM teaching the craft of composing to prize student Eric Johnson

Downtown music was also based on theories, but the theories (just notions to some) tended to be more random, often based on non-musical thinking. Zen-derived notes (John Cage and Chance); multi-media (e.g. Robert Ashley and operas based more on speaking than singing); Scoring via colors, pictograms and non-musical writings); Minimalism (Philip Glass and Steve Reich cum African rhythms); and of course Improvisation (non-jazz though jazz-influenced) were hallmarks of Downtown work. I lived in the Village and studied uptown at Juilliard and found my work becoming an amalgam and then something other-than Uptown and Downtown influences.

As critic I always tried to think and feel with the composer and at the same time with the performer. I added jazz and popular music criticism in a Voice column called NEW TIME, and intimate listening to those takes on music making added on yet more layers of creative crossover to my work. This was all fascinating and a beautiful challenge to an intellectually-hungry Midwesterner bent on finding excellence wherever it might live.

Recording with Taj Mahal and Allen Toussaint

While still a student there were occasionally sticky times when I'd find myself having to critique music and performances by my professors. Oh well...the facts, just the facts... This constant mega exposure to most of the music being performed in New York at the time not only enhanced my understanding, but also influenced my own compositional work. I lived downtown in the Village at the Judson Student House (where I met and married a nice Jewish woman named Susan Stern. Grandma loved her.) and studied uptown at Juilliard. Where to go creatively was the question.

Hall Overton had the answer. He had always taught me to learn broadly and exhaustively, then compose intuitively. This of course required a lot of trusting of the subconscious. But that's what I did. I began by joining in late-night improv sessions in Judson Church, often powering up the church organ and jamming with all manner of musicians who also wanted to create pieces intuitively (or just hang out with their axes). A flutist, a saxophonist (Terry Riley popped up there at least once), a percussionist or 2, a Jews harp player, somebody blowing into bottles, me on keyboards...we were all finding joy in bringing forth that strange series of musical crossover off-springs.

Of course how to really compose good music will always remain a mystery. There are many aspects of it that can be taught. Some are rules of thumb...some tricks of the trade...some are basic artistic principles...some even personal quirks. Maybe 1.) you write a little phrase that climbs up a few notes at the end, and you decide to repeat it a time or two. Generally to create a working statement based on repeats you should make a fourth time slightly different---maybe turning notes downward at the end. Or 2.) one is taught that you should be aware of the principle of contrasting sections in order to keep your listeners' ears freshened or in guessing mode. Or, as Overton taught, don't load up a piece with everything you know, and, as Berio taught, show at the beginning of a piece that you know what you're doing so the listener can settle back and realize he or she is in good hands for the rest of the piece. Or, as both Persichetti and Overton taught, always finish your piece excellently, because even if the rest of the piece has been wonderful, if you short-change the end, the last thing the listener hears is what that listener goes away with.

These and a ton of other "lessons" may be and should be taught to the composer. However, the thing that creates an unforgettable listening experience will almost always be some idea that floated up from your subconscious mind...strange, blinding flashes from somewhere inside? Or outside? As a fledgling composer, it was just those "strange" items that tended to embarrass me. They were unavoidably mine and beyond what people might have been hearing most of the time as "beautifully-crafted" or hip or "de rigueur." If people hearing it would pronounce it strange, it might cast aspersions on what might be inside you---foolishness or self-indulgence. You have to live awhile before not fearing to claim those licks which arise from "you-know-not whence." And when they come, you must get up out of your deepest sleep and write them down.

Performing on African flute at New York's Museum of Modern Art (late '70s)

COMPOSITIONAL SURVIVAL

Any creative artist can cite moments when they might have just hung the whole thing up. I've had a few, the first of it having come after my Composers Forum debut recital at New York's Donnell Library in the late '60s. I was definitely a new kid on the block. But I got together "A Movement for String Quartet," my "First Piano Sonata" (played brilliantly by David del Tredici, a friend whom I didn't know was a composer) and a piece called, I believe, "Wedding Cantata." My wife and I were invited subsequently to dinner at the home of Martin Mayer, a writer of best-selling books about doctors and lawyers, as well as a self-appointed music critic. Seated at dinner with him and his wife he casually announces, "We didn't like your music." Maybe casual for him, but a bomb to me—just a kid and stuck with him (I actually suspect his wife had liked my music) at least through dessert. That kind of stuff can be a career killer. I might have decided to drop composing and go into selling shoes or something, however the Herald Tribune critic the next day wrote a glowing review of the concert, and I took a deep breath and rolled on.

And I must say, I have suspected that racial stereotyping may have played a subtle part in keeping me out of the main halls of new music. I know of at least one occasion of a book being researched by a woman writer at Yale supposedly cataloguing the young composers on the scene. She wanted to be hip and include jazz, so she included (marvelous) Sam Rivers and then asked him for African-American names he might suggest. He told me to expect her call, but none materialized. I knew the woman and she knew me. My take is that she wanted Sam to suggest black jazz guys, not classicists. I thought of calling her on it, but in hindsight maybe it was a valuable thing for me. I soon basically disconnected from the legit classical world except when presenters or performers called me and requested work (which has happened a huge number of times over the years). Otherwise my approach has been to write exclusively what I like to hear and set up my own concerts and performance groups and continue on as if the new music scene was a figment of someone else's imagination. Of course already being a music critic didn't hurt.

CM instructing a student in Harlem

In 1968---with gracious advice from White composer Beatrice Witkin---Ben Patterson, Dorothy Rudd and Kermit Moore, Steven Chambers, and I formed The Society of Black Composers in New York and gave many first-rate concerts until 1973 when the heavy expenses of it all brought it to a halt. But while extant, The Society showcased such black classical composers as Noel Da Costa, Alvin Singleton, Olly Wilson, T.J. Anderson, and Dorothy Rudd Moore but as well highlighted such crossovers as David Baker, Leroy Jenkins, Ladji Camara, Herbie Hancock, and Ornette Coleman.

Sheridan Square/ Greenwich Village with some great First
Generation Village Voice critics and writers

<u>CITY BALLET</u>

Amazing how one thing may lead to another to another. I called poet W.H. Auden out of the blue one day and asked for an interview with him as a librettist, as he had just finished the libretto to an opera THE BASSARIDS scored by Hans Werner Henze. The opera was to be premiered that summer in Salzburg. Auden also happened to be my favorite living poet. He was living half his year nearby on St. Marks Place in the East Village and the other half in a village in Austria called Kirchstetten. An extremely gentle and phlegmatic gay Englishman with deep wrinkles and an enthusiastic taste for alcohol, he invited me over and offered me a drink. I graciously refused. As I entered I was surprised and impressed to find his television tuned to a basketball game. I took notes.

We became friends, and I was soon introduced to his friend Lincoln Kirstein, co-founder of the N.Y. City Ballet, who commissioned me to write a ballet score for Jacques D'Amboise, whom he'd hoped might become a choreographic great and rival George Balanchine. Dream on. I did write the score, called CATWALK, plus a bunch of fanfares for the new Saratoga summer festival. But a jealous enemy lurked in the form of the conductor of the City Ballet Orchestra. Besides being a hopeless alcoholic, he was a closet composer who'd shoot down anything new that he could this side of Stravinsky himself.

The orchestra did a reading of CATWALK one summer morning, and I naively held a tape recorder in my lap, recording the results so Jacques could have music against which to choreograph. Mister B listened in and said he liked what he heard. Kirstein whispered "You're going to be the next Stravinsky." But soon through that conductor's ministrations the recording was confiscated and destroyed ("union rules" said he), and my chance with City Ballet went down the tubes. Kirstein was furious and in tears as he wrote me a check for the commission. I didn't know what hit me. My wife Susan and I convalesced with a trip to Europe where we spent a couple delightful days with Auden and his partner Chester Kallman in Kirchstetten and several wondrous months in Italy at Berio's little stone house in the peasant village of Lingueglietta above the Riviera dei Fiori. Luciano needed to stay in New York that summer, so we traded our Columbus Avenue 4th floor-walk-up apartment for his little Italian domicile. Our first week in Lingueglietta we became friends with Luciano's mother, sister, and that whole family who lived in nearby Imperia. I played tennis frequently with Piero, Berio's brother-in-law who had led the group of Partigiani that captured Mussolini and Clara Petacci at the end of the War. While there, Berio's Alzheimer's-beset father died. Luciano was out of reach in America, and according to Italian tradition the widow was to have the son live with her for the week following the death. I and wife Susan were conscripted to live with delightful Mama Berio, a wonderful hostess and marvelous cook, in Luciano's stead. And this also called for a most unlikely scene---to whit, Carman Moore marching at the head of a long funeral parade, the widow on his arm, to the municipal burial grounds. Berio's father had been the local church organist and a well-regarded musician. A local, barely-in-tune band out of some movie played as we shuffled along, seriously crossed-over. Luciano showed up a few days later, and we shared an unforgettable week with him and his brilliant singer wife the late Cathy Berberian. One evening spent with them was at a disco in Milan which was fun until New York Beat poet Gregory Corso, who'd joined us, got drunk, climbed onto a table, loudly cursed Italy and found himself beat indeed...by some equally-inebriated Italian guys in the disco parking lot.

49

As a writer for the Voice I received a lot of notice and opportunities did spring forth. But the pittance of pay was not enough. My first son Martin popped out in 1968, and I was soon looking for employment. It was not long in coming. I was hired by a series of colleges, among them the Yale University School of Music, Queens and then Brooklyn Colleges (CUNY), Manhattanville College, Carnegie-Mellon, LaGuardia Community College, and The New School. And some of those teaching activities happened almost concurrently. In one 2 year stretch I each week taught at Yale for 2 days and then at Manhattanville the following day. And, mind you, at the same time I was writing SOMEBODY'S ANGEL CHILD; THE STORY OF BESSIE SMITH and going to concerts and writing my weekly Voice article, and---oh yes---composing. I not only felt tired all the time; I felt tarred. Being young does, however, get it done. I also worked in some tennis during warm weather, by the way. And it being the '60s, one had to get out and protest, as well. I was jailed (briefly) with a bunch of folks trying to integrate an amusement park in Baltimore. And with the same gang I marched on Washington frequently. It was exhilarating. It was enforced crossover. It was legal---sort of.

SIMULTANEOUS SYMPHONIES

**CM's new music class at Yale with
guest speaker B.B. King**

For a music orchestration class I was teaching at
The New School on Manhattan's 12th Street a
student named Peter Yarrow signed up and
occasionally showed up. That was, of course, the
Peter of Peter, Paul, and Mary and the writer of
"Puff, the Magic Dragon." Those teaching days
were heady, indeed. I got up my courage and
invited Frank Zappa to come talk to my New
School 20th Century music class, and lo and behold
show up he did. And he regaled us all with stories
and rock musical lore, after which he Pied Pipered

us all across the Village to attend the Mothers of Invention performance at the Fillmore East. So I became fast friends with both Zappa and Peter Yarrow (with whom I remain great friends). Through Peter I met famed conductor Seiji Ozawa who was his friend and was then conductor of the San Francisco Symphony. Seiji became intrigued by a piece for gospel singers and orchestra I was composing at the time called GOSPEL FUSE, and scheduled it for performance.

Amazing about the world of creative arts is that there are times when you bust your butt trying to get someone to schedule something of yours, and at other times things appear out of the blue, sometimes without your being anywhere near to ready. So always stay ready---whatever that means. Anyway, I went feverishly to work on my big gospel symphony. I found a way to meet with Aretha Franklin and both she and I planned for her to be the feature singer in it. But I soon found out about the firewall around so many of these star types, and I simply couldn't get to talk with her or even get a written message through any more. Being stupidly proud as well, I simply let it go and contacted the wonderful Cissy Houston, leader of Aretha's famed back-up group The Sweet Inspirations. It was an inspired choice. Cissy had more range and an incredible memory for pitch and rhythm. Then as I was finishing GOSPEL FUSE I received a totally-unexpected commission from Pierre Boulez and the New York Philharmonic. Quite in shock I went immediately to work on the piece, which became the 3-movement WILDFIRES AND FIELD SONGS. After a calming visit to my old Juilliard professor Vincent Persichetti I settled down and finished the work. I knew that GOSPEL FUSE was to have its premiere in San Francisco on Wednesday January 22, 1975. What I didn't know was that the N.Y. Philharmonic had scheduled the WILDFIRES premiere for the very next night Thursday January the 23rd, 1975. I loved it all, and I feared it all, knowing that I could have myself pelted with rotten eggs and tomatoes two nights in a row on two coasts. Moreover, the San Francisco piece was on a program with (my beloved) Haydn's Symphony #48, Mendelssohn's "Violin Concerto," and Bizet's "Roma,"and the N.Y. Phil piece was on with Mozart's "Concerto for Flute and Harp," De Falla's "Three-Cornered Hat Dances," and Stravinsky's "The Song of the Nightingale." Not to worry? Whew! Both pieces went beautifully.

**Receiving plaudits after New York Philharmonic premiere
of WILDFIRES AND FIELD SONGS**

LENNON

I was really getting to know and enjoy John, and suddenly he was gone.

I was conducting a pre-Skymusic group of instrumentalists reading from a score of mine requiring improvisation for a dance piece by Elaine Summers Dancers at NYU. Turned out John and Yoko were in the audience and loved what they heard. They invited me and Susan out for  coffee afterwards. We subsequently became friends and one evening all went to an Egyptian-oriented madness ("Rhoda in Potatoland"?) of Richard Foreman's in the West Village. John was at the time being hounded by Nixon's crew (allegedly for a pot possession thing back in England). You might think that he would be very cautious around that time. However at intermission I was talking to someone and felt a knock on the back o' me hand, smelled smoke, and looked around. It was John. Hmmm. Fearless guy. Sometime later I dropped by their little 2- room place in the West Village to interview Yoko about her then-new album. Turned on my tape machine and started in with John in the background sniping with ideas and corrections. We carried on with Yoko coming up with circus-like ideas for my page setting in the Voice as the tape ran down. As I was thanking Yoko and preparing to leave, smoke began to rise and John invited me to jam with him, an offer I could not refuse. So we began free-form improvising, me on their little pump organ and he on a big old acoustic guitar. Wish I would have recorded what we improvised. As I recall it was beautiful, but I can't prove it. The tape had been all used up with the interview. Months later I went as a character witness to his sham court appearance down on Centre Street. It was a quite comical proceeding as I remember it. John and I shared a few chuckles in the elevator on the way out. But the last time I saw and spoke with John was in the lobby of Avery Fisher Hall on January 23, 1975 before the New York Philharmonic would play the world premiere of WILDFIRES AND FIELD SONGS. John was dressed in a kind of Abe Lincoln suit with an Elvis Lives button on it.

"Do I look all right?" he asked (seriously). "Never been to one of these before." "You're spot on, John," I replied. Yoko, who'd appeared, Susan, John, and I group hugged and took off to our seats. Never saw him alive again.

THE SUNDANCE KID

Juilliard classmate and brilliant choreographer Martha Clarke hooked us up as a result of my complaining to her that I wasn't finding people to play serious tennis with. She reported that she knew two guys who might want to engage in racquet battles---one a writer and the other an actor. I chose the actor (thinking he might be trained in sword play or boxing or even modern dance and therefore might afford one some exercise). I discovered that he had been in "Barefoot in the Park," both on Broadway and in the film with Jane Fonda, and that he was about to film a Western. I also discovered that he hit pretty mean ground strokes. Pretty evenly-matched, we played our first tennis on the public courts in Central Park. But soon "Butch Cassidy and The Sundance Kid" hit the world screens, and public outings became not a good idea. Robert Redford became known. So from then on we played at private courts, outdoors and indoors as well.

I showed up one day in a bright blue warm-up suit, only to suffer all-American Redford's accusing me of looking like "Captain America." I knew then I'd truly crossed over---maybe a bit too far. The tennis rivalry got intense. He called to cancel a match one day because of a sudden business meeting, and I objected. "Carman, I can't blow off a meeting with the CEO of Gulf and Western because I've gotta play tennis," he countered. Meanwhile wife Susan and I became great friends with Bob and his wife Lola and hung out often. They were my balcony mates at the New York Philharmonic world premiere of WILDFIRES, and Redford frequently surprised me on my birthday with a meal or some event or another. At one such dinner a waiter came up all excited and exclaimed "I Spy…I Spy." We roared with laughter, realizing that he thought I was Bill Cosby and Redford must be Robert Culp. Sic transit Gloria.

N.Y. Philharmonic Orchestra concert, conducted by Pierre Boulez and featuring world-premiere of Moore's WILDFIRES AND FIELD SONGS. Robert Redford with wife Lola, Susan and Carman Moore with his mother and (partially-hidden) sister Claudette listening intently.

GOING HOME AGAIN('76)

The year following the bipartite GOSPEL FUSE/WILDFIRES AND FIELD SONGS symphonic splash was 1976 and the U.S. Bicentennial. All around the country towns were trying to figure out how to celebrate. Elyria, Ohio had me, a local who'd appeared with picture not only in the New York Times but more importantly to them in People and Newsweek Magazines. And so it was that I was called home and presented with a commission to create a celebration piece. I dived in and decided on something that would involve the locals... high school choirs, bands, and orchestras, a local jazz combo, a gospel singer, and the owner of Elyria's own Universal Joint Auto Wrecking...a guy with a great speaking voice.

I called it THE GREAT AMERICAN NEBULA (which the nice ladies guiding the project first pronounced as ne-BU-la, perhaps thinking it Swahili or Yoruba or something). The local Elyria Chronicle Telegram was full of pictures and announcements of the concert all week. One prominently-placed photo was of me smiling alongside several ladies from the Elyria Daughters of The American Revolution chapter...ladies who seemed to be only trying to smile. My wonderful Skymusic pianist Eric Johnson flew out to help with rehearsals, and we rehearsed everybody to the nines for days. The concert took place in the high school gym, was packed, and was an enormous success. The kids sang and played like angels, and Nelson Beller narrated like Walter Cronkite. But for me the highlight of the evening occurred before I took the podium.

Koste Belcheff, the Elyria bandmaster and actually a fellow OSU music school alum, introduced me warmly and topped it all by having my dear Grandma Franklin wheeled out for applause. Surprised, I almost lost it right there. She smiled and waved regally to the crowd. One of my life's biggest debts was getting paid off. Needless to say, as I took the podium and gave the downbeat, a special spark was lit for that performance. The reception after the concert was held at the Country Club, a place where blacks once could go only to caddy.

C.M. with mother and gracious Elyria, Ohio hosts at Country Club reception after premiere of Bicentennial commissioned work THE GREAT AMERICAN NEBULA.

THE SKYMUSIC ENSEMBLE

From the humble beginnings of Judson Church night-time improvisation sessions came a realization that improv plus some Uptown-style on-the-page-scored planning might yield some truly unusual work. In any event being at Judson meant being around a bunch of major chance-takers. The church is located right on Washington Square Park in Greenwich Village, and soon after I arrived there from the sticks Judson was the rescue spot for guitar twangers and bongo bangers being billy-clubbed in the famed Folk Music Riots of 1961. Actual blood dripped from actual heads of kids insisting on playing folk tunes out-loud around the public space of the Square's fountain without a police permit, and I witnessed it. Dylan and others were in the Park in those days creating history rather than a ruckus, but...well you know...guess that's what history being made often looks like. Anyway, it caused me to tremble, but I knew which side I would be on---for life. But I digress—sort of.

Also at Judson was the nascent Judson Dancers group, whose work was in protest against pretty dance, consciously artistic dance, and traditional dance costumery (some dancing without any costume at all). Such choreographers as Yvonne Rainer, Elaine Summers, Carolee Schneemann, Steve Paxton, and Trisha Brown also seemed to be carefully avoiding on-page planning and any taint of masterpiece seeking (hanging around Judson at the time were also such visual artists as Robert Rauschenberg, Jim Dine, and Claes Oldenberg and any number of Happeners).

So as I lived at the Judson Student House which adjoined the church, there was no way that I would not create something advanced and unusual in that space. I started organizing a real group based around my ragtag gang of improvisers, but a music group that could read scores and follow my conducting, even if it might be out-of-step with the hard-core Judson crowd. It had to be, because I was first of all shy, and then not a crack instrumentalist nor even a true performing artist. All I could do was compose and conduct, so if I wanted to hear my music in that world it would have to be sounded forth by accomplices.

Thus came to be the group which I at first called The Interplayers and finally The Skymusic Ensemble. Actually the proto-group came together out of Elaine Summers' need for music for her new idea of "intermedia," a form she devised which would always require three art forms intertwined---those of dance, film, and music. She herself being a choreographer and film-maker had the first two nailed. So by meeting me and liking what she'd heard from my improv experiments, she made the Skymusic idea an absolute necessity by constantly asking me for music. In 1972 my rag-tag Interplayers journeyed with Elaine's dance group to London for the week-long ICES (International Carnival of Experimental Sound) Festival. It worked because composer friends Alvin Singleton and Steve Dickman happened to be in Europe on Fulbright Scholarships and flutist Robert Cram was traveling there and I was able to talk them into coming to Britain to join our merry improv-laced adventure. Talent won out, and we were well-received---at least that's how I remember it.

A friend of Elaine's, jazz-great Sam Rivers happened to be one of the finest musicians on the planet, so once back in Gotham I grabbed him and anointed him Skymusician Number One, to soon be joined by pioneering synthesizer artist Kenneth Bichel, my composition student and brilliant keyboardist Eric Johnson, flute virtuoso Kitty Hay, percussionist extraordinaire Gordon Gottlieb, and piano virtuoso and Juilliard teacher Marianna Rosett. Alvin Singleton hooked me up with the wild violinist and former AACM force Leroy Jenkins, and suddenly I had a world-beating group of musicians---each with widely-divergent styles, but all of whom could read my scribbly scores and improvise brilliantly. Being a Libra, I was able to create scores that mediated everyone's style and milk everyone's best and most natural for the cause of good music making.

With Ken Bichel, Kitty Hay, Marianna Rosett, and Leroy Jenkins in Piazza San Marco, Venice, New Years Eve on the way to play at La Scala in Milan.

In 1980 the Ensemble was asked by Cathedral of St. John the Divine's Dean James Parks Morton to join such characters as Philippe Petit and Paul Winter in becoming Cathedral Artists-in-Residence. The residency allowed us performance opportunities in one of the world's most enormous spaces. From there over the years the Ensemble has performed world-wide, including at La Scala Opera House in Milan where I conducted them in my score to Alvin Ailey's LA DEA DELLE ACQUE ---choreographed by him for the Ballet Company of La Scala the year before he died.

Of course I'd made the mistake of providing Alvin with a CD of the work the way we do things, which meant embellished with improvisations. The first rehearsal with the ballet company was an Italian madhouse. First of all the crew in the orchestra pit had never had a synthesizer there, so they wanted to slice up Eric's synth and wire it into the theatre's main system. "No, no, no, just a regular wall plug, please," we exclaimed. Then from the dancers, "Where is that zing boom boom in the 19th measure of the 2nd Section of the...? etc., etc...." they were asking. So that very night I and all the musicians, instead of laughing and idling over great Italian wine, had to sit down and recreate the whole piece with every bang, breath, and tremolo of improv on the CD in place. No sleep, but we did it! And the critics after the premiere performance shouted "hurray" or its equivalent. Anyway, we'd earned our Chianti. And Alvin pleased me greatly when he exclaimed," we're going to work a lot together." But he died soon after.

Backstage at La Scala Opera House with Skymusicians Leroy Jenkins, Marianna Rosett, Ken Bichel (Wendy his wife), and Gordon Gottlieb (1989).

ISAIAH JACKSON/
DANCE/ THEATRE

So it was the '80s/'90s, and life had its hectic spells.
I found myself overworked and divorced. My work
alternated between good old-fashioned written-out
symphonic and chamber music and Skymusic-style
creations for specific musicians who thrived in a
part-written out/part-improvised scenario. Many of
the orchestral works were conducted by the gifted
Isaiah Jackson, with a series of orchestras including
the   Cleveland   Orchestra,   the   Rochester
Philharmonic, the Dayton Philharmonic, and the
Virginia Symphony. I'd first met African-American

Maestro Jackson in 1976 when he conducted my 4 MOVEMENTS FOR A FASHIONABLE 5-TOED DRAGON with the Orchestra of the Sorbonne in Hong-Kong for their Ready-to-Wear fashion spectacular (is that enough crossing over, or what…?). Besides becoming a life-long friend he also premiered "HIT; A CONCERTO FOR PERCUSSION AND ORCHESTRA" and "TO THE POWER OF PEACE," and gave sparkling 2nd and 3rd performances of many of my works."

With Mom and Maestro Isaiah Jackson after Cleveland Orchestra performance of GOSPEL FUSE Severance Hall

Among Isaiah's orchestral posts was that of Music Director of England's Royal Ballet Company. But a terrible affliction to his inner ear mechanism has since put an end to this gifted conductor's career in music. When the American Dance Festival engaged me as Music Director of

their Young Choreographers in Residence Project in
'86 at Duke University, I began to write dance
scores in earnest. Following the City Ballet miscue
I had created dance music for Anna Sokolow
(MEMORIES, which she never finished), Garth
Fagan (SALON), Martha Clarke (SEAN SEAN),
and a few others. But the Ailey and ADF stretches
got me deep into modern dance. Scores for Donald
Byrd, Mark Dendy, Ruby Shang, Cleo Parker
Robinson, Sang-cheul Choi, Michiyo Sato, Kiori
Kawai, Eun-mi Cho, Hey-Jeong Yoon and the
American Tap Dance Orchestra's Brenda Buffalino
followed at a dizzying pace.   I loved it and
discovered how really fast (and carefully) I can
compose. And although I had typically written my
own libretti and words to songs, close friendships
with writers such as Ishmael Reed, Colleen
McElroy, and Charles "OyamO" Gordon soon
pulled me into writing for theatre.

One early result was WILD GARDENS OF THE
LOUP GAROU, a mega-crossover setting of poems
chosen from Ishmael and Colleen's works for 4
singing actors---2 black and 2 white...2 women and
2 men...with a plot set in a post-Vietnam War
never-neverland.   Another was Ishmael's opera
libretto GETHSEMANE PARK concerning New
Testament   characters   (including   Satan)   as
contemporary people, the Homeless against the
Taxpayers and typical Ish societal mishugoss (he
dubbed the form a "gospera"). To OyamO libretti I
have set a children's musical THE SORCERER'S

69

APPRENTICE for the Seattle Children's Theatre; DISTRAUGHTER a comedy concerning a panda-bear cult; CLUB PARADISE, Milton's "Paradise Lost" set in a dance club; and the upcoming WHITE HOT BLACK SPICE set in 1917 New Orleans Storyville. And I have also set Seamus Heaney's Antigone creation THE BURIAL AT THEBES and Lella Heins' children's musical ORIUNDINA, set in Brazil's Bahia. I have enjoyed immensely working with these masters of the written word, but I also like to write my own lyrics and libretti. With all the experience gained with the afore-named and with the year 2000 looming, I decided to create a large work with spiritual meaning and words by myself. That work was to be MASS FOR THE 21ST CENTURY.

**CM and Charles "OyamO" Gordon at the First
Annual Black Literary Marketplace Expo, April 2011**

MASS FOR THE 21ST CENTURY

I do have the notion that working in the depths of the creative arts renders the artist a naturally spiritual person. The constant experience of discovery, surprise at what keeps coming forth from oneself, plus familiarity with flat-out miracles just makes it unavoidable. I feel that since the first Homo Sapiens and the Cave Days, those of us gifted with extra helpings of artistic feel and vision were meant to be priests of the tribe and creators of music, especially, have direct links to Universal Creation. This is not just a gift, it is a duty.

And so it was with the advice of seeker friend Billielee Mommer that I, though no Catholic nor

Episcopalian, decided to create a mass for the upcoming Millennium to be called MASS FOR THE 21ST CENTURY. I had no money to speak of. This mass would be a spiritual spokes vehicle for all religions and even un-religions. I examined every point of spiritual common ground and came up with all the words needed for this piece.

Ensemble triumphant in Geneva, soon to be recruited as MASS "orchestra"

After a wonderful afternoon spent discussing the traditional mass with Dean Morton of the Cathedral, I felt ready to begin work. This piece would be an example of new wine in an old bottle, mass in form only, a mass for the world masses, expressed in Arabic, Latin, English, Lakota or whatever language necessary as it travels the world and is translated in both words and local custom. Muslims,

Christians, Jews, Hindus, Buddhists...all could enthusiastically sing "grant us peace" or "glory to god" or "lord, have mercy" and add "we celebrate as One." I went looking for a librettist to word this thing, but while waiting found my subconscious bombarded with words that demanded to be set to music. And the music appeared almost simultaneously. Soon there was no room for anyone else's words or music. This work was to be, and now is, an international ritual of crossover.

When something is supposed to happen, the right people are always in the right place at the right time. It was 1994. Lincoln Center just happened to have as director of its Out-of-Doors Festival a friend of Elaine Summers' and an enormously perceptive and visionary person named Jenneth Webster. When I proposed the Mass to her for the Festival, she got it immediately. Granted, it would require enormous forces—an adult choir, a children's choir, 4 solo concert singers, 2 gospel singers (one of them Cissy Houston mother of Whitney), a Senegalese griot, an instrumental group, a dance company, some mimes, a limber in-line skater, 10 authentic religious figures, and costumes. But Jenneth understood the importance of the piece, got it scheduled, and got me commissioned to finish composing it. We rehearsed this grand group and gave 2 performances, enthusiastically received by over 10,000 audience members. MASS FOR THE 21ST CENTURY lives, and I know it will be brilliantly recorded and performed long after I have shuffled off this mortal coil.

**CM and MASS FOR THE 21ST CENTURY dancers
at Lincoln Center 1994 taking bows**

POST-MASS DEPRESSION

After the big Lincoln Center performances, I realize now, I should have followed up on the excitement and natural momentum it had generated and gone after more performances elsewhere and a serious recording. But I was broke paying off a gang of things, and more immediately I was exhausted both physically and mentally. By the end of the final (2 hours and 20 minute) performance my conducting arm began cramping and went into such a spasm that I had to finish the work left-handed. I felt finished-off, but I was not finished. Maybe I was noticing a self-defeat mechanism within me. I thought back to having let myself get pushed out of the City Ballet situation. Maybe I should have fought that conductor before dropping the matter. I thought back to letting Aretha get away from GOSPEL FUSE, even though Cissy Houston had been spectacular. And I remembered that following the successful GOSPEL FUSE premiere, perhaps stuck in some '60s anti-Establishmentarian fog, I'd refused to sign a recording contract for the work offered by Deutsche Grammophon. And now the non follow-up with the MASS. I was broke and my lack of business sense was overwhelming me. It was as if things outside music itself were always going too fast for me. Maybe a valuable lesson about momentum was starting to press itself upon me. Either way I just wanted to compose.

Following that event of 1994 my first large-scale work didn't occur until my 2002 children's opera RASUR was commissioned and performed to great applause for a week in Costa Rica. Set in Spanish, RASUR concerns a legendary Costa Rican Indian forest spirit who, along with forest animals, helps the children of 2 warring villages bring peace into the world of their belligerent parents. It was full of songs and choruses for adult and child performers, was accompanied by a national symphony orchestra, and had the backing of the government. RASUR like the MASS needs future performances and a definitive recording.

Also during this period I wrote the first words for a fellow composer since those for Felix Cavaliere's 2 solo albums in the 1970's, when I created a libretto for my life-long colleague and fellow African-American classical crossover guy

Alvin Singleton. The work is a choral/dance work called TRUTH and treats the life of the great Abolitionist and women's rights fighter Sojourner Truth. Commissioned and premiered by Minneapolis' Vocal Essence Choir, it was a major success for all concerned.

My compositional work subsequent to that has been deeply influenced by the coming of electronic equipment, not least the computer and digital software that has helped me efficiently and quickly copy scores and parts. But my very best friend has been my Ensoniq electronic keyboard with built-in memory and gorgeous sounds which can be multi-tracked in sweet concord with one another. The timing of this keyboard's appearance in my life couldn't have been more apt. Playing tennis in California without warming up that summer I tore my right Achilles tendon and faced months of sitting around. So I sat around with the Ensoniq's enormous manual and gave my right brain a bit of a rest. I then followed those weeks and months of that brand of cogitation with hours and hours of improvising all manner of pieces both long and short. Many of these were meditative ones of great personal value in keeping my mind quiet and my Achilles healing. One of the gifts of that period was discovering a way to deploy musical events that could move notes around the listener's body (chakras), sometimes playing on the forehead, sometimes probing the groin, sometimes pushing deep into the solar plexus, sometimes tickling the eyelids...all this while constructing harmonies and melodies "as usual" and still taking you on the adventure that a real piece of music demands.

Anyway, once I had made hundreds of these Ensoniq keyboard pieces (most with no names to this very day) I found myself back at work on building large orchestral and choral pieces also mocked-up on the synthesizer. Among these have been CONCERTO FOR FLUTE, PI'PA, AND ORCHESTRA and CONCERTO FOR ORNETTE AND ORCHESTRA. Paucity of funds has held up the world premieres of both of these worthy works.

ORNETTE

Several years back I became friends with the King of Crossover---by name, one Ornette Coleman. Ornette's main instrument is alto saxophone, and he also plays others, among them violin, which he plays untraditionally---fingering with the right hand and sawing with the left. Some years ago I found myself with a small group of folks recruited to come to his Soho loft and sing and record his rockish tune called "Friends And Neighbors (That's Where It's At)". I am by no stretch a singer, although when I sing I sing in tune and on time under easy circumstances (Once sang "We Shall Overcome" on Louis Armstrong's 70th birthday album LOUIS ARMSTRONG AND HIS

FRIENDS).   So I sang, and maybe my having traveled that extra vocal mile for him cemented our palhood.

Anyway, Ornette and I are waiting for the next opportunity of orchestra and funds to perform and record the CONCERTO. And while waiting, he and I have been getting together frequently to listen to music and play 8-ball pool on his big table.   He loves it, in no small part because I suck at pool.   I really am mainly fascinated watching the balls click and zip madly around the place.   But it ain't tennis.

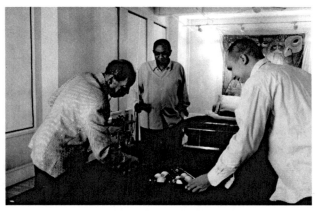

**Ornette Coleman, Carman, and son
Martin—caballeros all**

SO NOW?

Though not getting any younger chronologically, fresh projects keep thrusting new spring times upon me. Several new chamber works, among them SHE (AN APPRECIATION) and HIGH HEAVENS (for Skymusic) are being heard. A new musical WHITE HOT BLACK SPICE has been dropped onto my workbench by cousin OyamO its librettist (realizing I almost never say no to anything these days). With jazz vocal great Janet Lawson I have written a jazz history wrapped in an adventure story for kids called GRANDMA SAGE AND HER MAGIC MUSIC ROOM, as yet unpublished. And with renewed energy I am leading The Skymusic Ensemble back onto the world stage. Also among very special recent career arrivals has been the gift of my Maine friend, extreme music lover, and attorney Kyle Jones---a summer music festival in my name. Called The Carman Moore New Music Festival it is being held on Maine's beautiful Mount Desert Island every August and features all manner of crossover music from rock to extreme classical. All I need do is show up and bless the thing. Y'all come. Wow!

But maybe the chief new item in the crossover department is the rock'n'roll concept album DANTE ROCKS or THE LEGEND OF DON AND BEA. Dante, perhaps the major conceiver of the notion of Renaissance love back in the 14th Century, is someone whose thought and poetry (e.g. as iterated in THE DIVINE COMEDY) have consumed me for a long time. Somehow I decided that an opera about it all wouldn't quite afford enough kick. A rocking DON AND BEA posits the notion of Beatrice flying into Time/Space via the Big Bang chased by a desperately lovelorn Dante in a rickety space ship. The songs (concept, lyrics and some tune collaborations by me) take them both from Infernal to Purgatorial to Paradisiacal and in the process get this Dante fixation off my chest. Premik, Charles Burnham, and Elliott Randall (once of Steely Dan) all play splendid solos on the album's 10 songs. Jessica Seidel and Jason Hill are our Bea and Don.

So I get to crossover into the world of popular art once again...the recording studios...the rhythm section and the stringent vocalizing...the sound effects and the final mixing. These all appeal mucho. A rock album? I'm not trained for it: Therefore I Am.

Otherwise I live simply and in a routinized manner. I enjoy the out-and-out work of composing music---and writing lyrics. I love hitting tennis balls. I love women. I love my friends and family. And I love taking long walks, both on the City streets where the free show never closes and as well in Central Park.

CENTRAL PARK

I've lived just one block away for many years...so many that I've come to regard the place as my own...my back yard with its own meadows and woods and lakes and rocks and wildlife. Nobody has ever contradicted me on that, so I persist.

I cross the traffic of Central Park West and disappear into the Park, like to a lover. As I go deeper and deeper in, things grow reliably quieter and quieter...all seasons. In the seasons surrounding winter they also grow greener and greener, cleaner and cleaner. Car noises fall away and give way to bird songs and the chirping of little kids. In summer the temperature drops the further in you go. Perhaps the most enlightened action by a city government in history, Olmsted and Vaux's masterpiece is an everyday raving success in an unassuming kind of way. Billionaires and the homeless get equalized as its medicinal magic lays balm on all.

Personally I run most every day in the Park in the morning and maybe walk another time in the afternoon and yet once more at night. Every spot feels and looks different every time of every day....like a great piece of music, familiar but never the same. I delight in the sensation of being able to in effect travel in and out of the City in minutes, simply by crossing the street. Once in, I admire and know many specific trees and specific rocks. I usually choose to disappear into the Ramble and leave people behind as a simple act of will. So the Park is my secret, and yes, I totally realize that it is and has been the secret of millions of fellow New Yorkers for over a century and a half. How many pieces of music, books, plays, and articles, ideas for paintings and creative photographs have been the gift of that big old all-embracing green mama over the years? I can only speak for myself. Most of what I create has some Central Park engraved upon it. I'd be honored to take my final walk on the planet in Central Park.

Central Park

SPIRITUAL MATTERS

My Grandpa Franklin used to mutter to himself with great frequency, "thank you, Jesus." I didn't get it then, but I know now what he was saying. I say the essence of it all the time. It bespeaks a spiritual practice rooted in pure gratitude. Love and help others, (not forgetting yourself) human and beyond and express your wonder at what you experience through gratitude. And the core of that gratitude is "thanks for equipping me to notice those wonders."

My own religious persuasion has thus been self-assembled through life experiences. And I remain open to expanding it, shortening it, or even replacing it, if it is felt. I have no real idea how we're here and what that's all about. All I know is that I admire what I see and frequently feel enormous inner pressure to burst out with thank yous---even for horrors, pains, personal poverty and impenetrable mysteries. And the Park is my priest, imam, and rabbi. Winter freezes and summer sears. Fall and spring cross over. All together they add up to raw beauty. It's hard not to notice.

I know it is God---the real thing. But I feel the word God has been so corrupted and diminished that, as the late great philosopher, Jesuit Thomas Berry had it, "I think we need to rest the word "God" for awhile and let it recover its true meaning." The wide-open conceptual world of Lao-tse's Tao gives me most of what my spirit needs in appreciating the totality that is the truth of God. I have a simple definition of Tao/God/Allah, etc. that sees it as no more and no less than "All That There Is." And I feel that this One observes, loves, appreciates, and knows itself with the help of the eyes and ears of all beings including you and me, our cells and of the burning galaxies. As a composer of music I feel treated beyond pure chance with ideas, energy, and miracles. And so I believe that both my music and my walks in the Park, where I feel conversed with, are holy. And yet I have no idea what's really going on.

I suspect that beyond our Universe of time/space, yin/yang, AC vibration duality the Tao has "many mansions" and whole other ways of being. But all I can (just barely) handle is this Universe of vibrations and my portion---music.

Of course maybe it's all Music.
I'm comfortable with a crossover like that.
....
And so this book, **CROSSOVER**? It is a "Who-Am-I?" bio of exploration, written by someone who is terminally curious.

ABOUT THE AUTHOR

**Carman Moore, like America, a crossover/
Because of America, a crossover.**

Carman Moore is a world-renowned Composer and
Conductor, Author, and Music Critic. A dedicated
educator, Moore has taught at the Yale University
School of Music, Queens and Brooklyn Colleges,
Carnegie-Mellon University, Manhattanville
College, and New School University. He is
presently creating a pop music album based in
Outer Space and featuring Dante and Beatrice for
the new SKYBAND. He has recently completed
CONCERTO FOR ORNETTE AND ORCHESTRA
for jazz legend and 2006 Pulitzer prize award
winner Ornette Coleman. Particularly interested in
reaching out to children, he spent several years in
the 1960's, 70's and 80's as a teaching artist for
Lincoln Center and Jazzmobile and at The Dalton
School. Moore conducted his work and lectured in
New York public schools with the Lincoln Center
Institute, which commissioned his The Magic Turn
Around Town and Save the Dragon. In 1995 he
served as consultant to Wynton Marsalis on his
popular PBS-broadcast home video series for
children, Marsalis On Music. Moore is also the
author of two youth-oriented books: Somebody's
Angel Child: The Story of Bessie Smith (Dell), and

Rock-It (a music history and theory book for Alfred Music Publishers). With celebrated jazz vocalist Janet Lawson he has written GRANDMA SAGE AND HER MAGIC MUSIC ROOM, an adventure story for children that is also a history of jazz. He has served as Board member and adjudicator for several major organizations, including Composers Forum, the Society of Black Composers, the N.Y. State Council on the Arts, and the National Endowment for the Arts. In addition he has been music critic and columnist for the Village Voice and has contributed to The New York Times, The Saturday Review of Literature, Vogue, and Essence among others.

SOME PEOPLE INTERVIEWED and MET:

STEVIE WONDER
JERRY WEXLER
ALVIN AILEY
WYNTON MARSALIS
SONNY ROLLINS
B.B. KING
YOKO ONO
JOHN LENNON
ERROLL GARNER
RAY BARRETTO
LA LUPE
FELIX CAVALIERE
VIRGIL THOMSON
ORNETTE COLEMAN
ROBERT REDFORD
W.H. AUDEN
GEORGE BALANCHINE
EARL "THE PEARL" MONROE
THELONIOUS MONK
JERRY LEIBER/MIKE STOLLER
FRANK ZAPPA
ANNA SOKOLOW
LINCOLN KIRSTEIN

JOHN HAMMOND
MAVIS STAPLES
WILSON PICKETT
TINA TURNER
JACK GEE
LOUIS ARMSTRONG

PHOTO JOURNAL

**CM in 2000 Who's Who Millennium photo of major
American composers in New York City**

CM with a pride of American Composers

Conducting and recording saxophone great Sam Rivers

CM with record producer Bob Thiele and Louis the Magnificent at Louis Armstrong's 70th birthday surprise party and recording session. Present were Miles Davis, Ornette Coleman, Tony Bennett, George Wein, Oliver Nelson, and Chico Hamilton. We all joined in as a choir to record "We Shall Overcome" with Louis Armstrong. Imagine that!

Modern dance legendary choreographer Anna Sokolow for whom CM composed MEMORIES

CM at premiere of Sojourner Truth choral drama TRUTH in St. Paul. CM (librettist) and composer Alvin Singleton flank Alvin's publisher Norman Ryan.

CM with jazz critic Gary Giddins and PEN official Elizabeth Weinstein

CM with Henry Threadgill, James Jordan, Tania Leon, and Ornette Coleman at Judson Church after a memorial for legendary composer and Skymusic violinist Leroy Jenkins.

CM at post-concert reception

Skymusic Ensemble members in Hong Kong after performing FOUR MOVEMENTS FOR A 5-TOED DRAGON with the Orchestra of the Sorbonne--- Ken Bichel (keyboards), Elliott Randall (guitar), and Warren Smith (percussion). Missing are Sam Rivers (saxophone) and Richard Davis (bass).

Appreciating Sri Chinmoy

Being appreciated by Sri Chinmoy

CM at 2010 G20 Ethics and Spirituality Conference

**With Sr. Sun-ok Lee and friends
G20 in Korea 2010**

With friends at G20 in Korea 2010

**CM on sacred grounds of Korea's Won Buddhists crossing
over with fellows of G20 "Moral Politics" Summit 2010**

99

**CM leads arts fellows to pasta feast at Civitella Ranieri
Castle in Umbria, Italy; May 2010**

**With Susan Moore at the Philharmonic premiere of
WILDFIRES AND FIELD SONGS**

Yoko Ono

101

ROBERT REDFORD

April 11, 2007

Carman Moore
152 Columbus Ave., #4R
New York, NY 10023

Carman –

You ol' dog. How good to hear from
you. And to receive your generous "Quiet
Music" clips. Would love to catch up – and yes
I still bang the balls around despite an annoying
arthritic grip. I will probably do it until I drop.

I do hope to see you. I come in to New
York 6 – 8 times a year. I have an office there

And cheers to Kyle Jones for recognition
of your worth.

All the best,

Bob

5/16/72

Dear Common,

forgive me for not answering sooner, but I would very much like to <u>hear</u> the <u>tune</u> the word's and the thought are <u>terrific</u>

(2)
Should you arrange for the necessary musicians + soloist for a demonstration Record for me, I would like to know the cost + Absorb it for you, don't you think it's worth it! (As soon as possible) I think now is the time for such a release! Please leave your reply with Larue Manon's 489 1400 - Queen's booking.
Sincerest + warm Regards

P.S. I could probably arrange a deduction for studio time ~~through~~ though Atlantic Records.

+ phone No.

1972 - Note from Aretha Franklin

Playing and singing for old pal the late Leonard Marks, who suffered from Alzheimer's.

CM with fellow composers Steven Paulus, Nick Demos, and Alex Shapiro, post-concert.

**Big Skyband recording session—For That Dante &
Beatrice-In-Outer-Space Album...**

**Dante recording session lead singer
Jessica Seidel and bassist Brian**

Dante bass man Brian

CM pondering changes at the Dante session

Dante session sound engineer Mike White and guests

**CM with pianist Eric Johnson after
Dante rockin' recording session**

AmericanComposer

Carman

by Kyle Gann

2006 - Chamber Music Magazine

Double Header

Griffith (right), contrarians Byron

1994 – Newsweek Magazine

The New York Times

NEW YORK, FRIDAY, AUGUST 12, 1994

MUSIC REVIEW

A Composer's Vision of a Perfect World

By ALLAN KOZINN

Mor Dior Seck and Cynthia Heller performing in Carman Moore's "Mass for the 21st Century" on Wednesday night as part of the Lincoln Center Out of Doors festival.

August 12, 1994 - By ALLAN KOZINN - Weekend Desk

Before Leaving the 20th Century, Listening to It

By JAMES R. OESTREICH

The composer Carman Moore conducting a rehearsal of his "Mass for the 21st Century," with his Skymusic ensemble, at the J

'It was clear that it had to be about the children.'

August 9, 1994 - By JAMES R. OESTREICH

2002 - CM's children's opera RASUR premiered in Costa Rica

2002 - CM's children's opera RASUR premieres in Costa Rica

Carman Moore's morning walk in Central Park

CPSIA information can be obtained at www.ICGtesting.com
Printed in the USA
LVOW030810041011

249026LV00013B/11/P

9 781877 807794